If you can change your mind, you can change your life.

Plans to give you hope and a future

Jeremia 29:11

The
Lord
is my
light
and my
salvation

Psalm 27:1

He cares for you.

1 Peter 5: 7

Trust in the Lord with all your heart

Proverbs 3:5

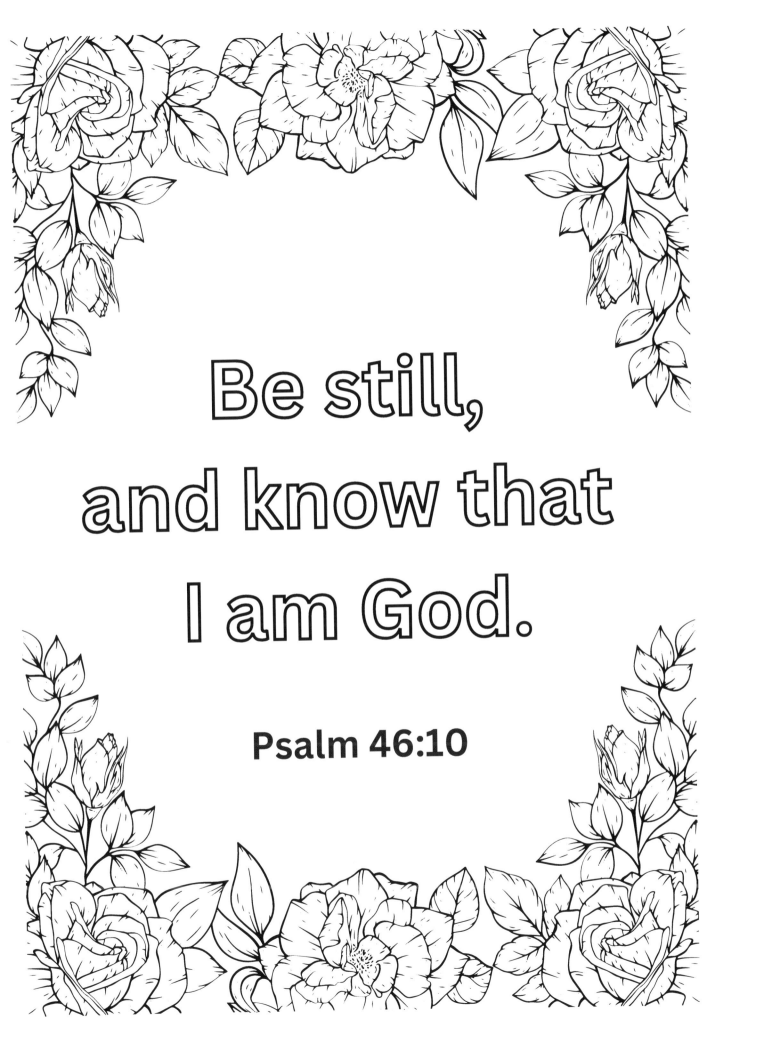

Be still, and know that I am God.

Psalm 46:10

I will never
leave you

nor
forsake
you

Hebrews 13:5

He cares for those who trust in him.

Nahum 1:7

The Lord is my rock, my fortress, and my deliverer.

Psalm 18:2

He heals the brokenhearted.

Psalm 147:3

I am the way and the truth and the life

John 14:16

The joy of the Lord is my strenght.

Nehemiah 8:10

Come to me and I will give you rest.
Matthew 11:28

The Lord
is my strenght
and my shield

Psalm 28:7

Do not be afraid, for I am with you.

Isaiah 41:10

The new creation has come, The old has gone.

2 Corinthians 5:17

The Lord is faithful

2 Thessalonians 3:3

Don't let yesterday take up too much of today.

The Lord is my shepherd.

Psalm 23:1

Embrace your journey

Gift of God
is eternal life.
Romans 6:23

Don't watch the clock, do what it does. Keep going...

The Lord will fight for you, you need only to be still.

Exodus 14:14

Keep your focus, dream big and dare to fail.

The Lord is my light and my salvation

Psalm 27:1

Small positive thought in the morning, can change your whole day

Trust in the Lord with all your heart
Proverbs 3:5-6

Opportunities don't just happen, you create them.

For those who love God, all things work together for good.

Romans 8:28

Don't let someone else's opinion of you become your reality.

If you're not positive energy, you're negative energy.

Fear not,
for I am with you.

Isaiah 41:10

Come to me and I will give you rest.
Matthew 11:28

Do what you can, with what you have, where you are.

Be strong...

God is with you wherever you go.

Joshua 1:9

If you can dream it,
you can do it.

He gives power to the weak and strength to the powerless.

Isaiah 40:29

The Lord is my helper
I will not fear

Hebrews 13:6

You cannot always control what goes on outside,

But, you can control what goes on inside.

This is the day that the Lord has made

Psalm 118:24

If there is no struggle there is no progress

Let not your hearts be troubled; Believe in God.

John 14:1

Courage is like a muscle

We strengthen it by use

Start where you are

Use what you have

Do what you can

God is good, all the time
All the time, God is good.

A joyful heart is good medicine

Proverbs 17:22

You'll never get bored when you try something new. There's really no limit to what you can do.

Now, may the Lord of peace himself give you peace at all times in every way.

2 Thessalonians 3:16

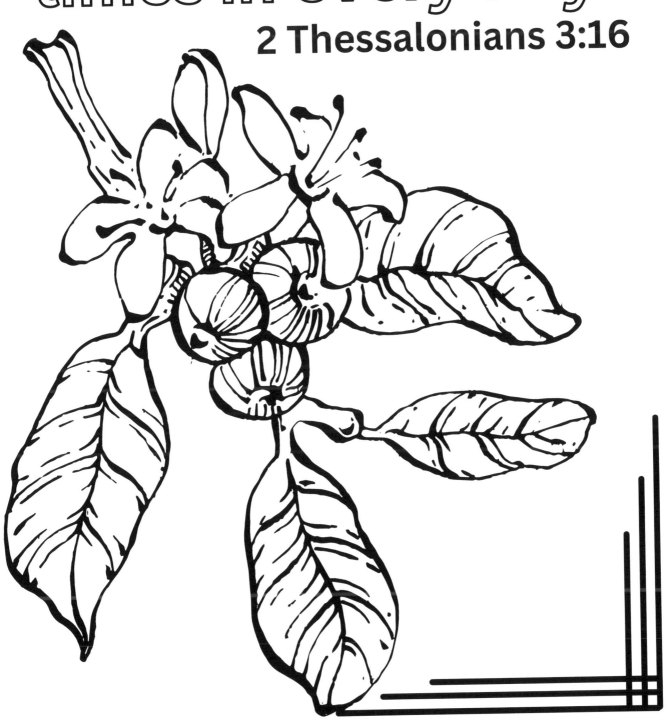

Self care isn't selfish

The Lord is my rock and my salvation

Psalm 18:1-2

I am the vine; you are the branches.

John 15:5

You got this

For we walk by faith, not by sight.
2 Corinthians 5:7

It takes courage
to grow up

Bless the Lord, O my soul.

Psalm 103:1-2

Your self-worth is determined by you,

don't depend on someone telling you who you are

Fear not, I am the one who helps you

Isaiah 41:13

You are the one, who'll decide where to go.

Give thanks to the Lord

Psalm 107:1

Never too late
to set another goal
or a new dream

Be still, and know that I am God.

Psalm 46:10

If you risk nothing

then
you risk everything

Just don't give up trying to do what you really want to do

Ask, and it will
be given
to you;
seek, and
you will find.
Knock,
and
it will be opened
to you.

Matthew 7:7

In God I trust
I shall not be afraid

Psalm 56:4

Optimism is a happiness magnet

Problem is a chance for you to do your best

Seek first the kingdom of God and his righteousness, and all things will be added on to you.

Matthew 6:33

Give thanks and bless his name. For the Lord is good

Psalm 100:4-5

Doubt kills
more dreams
than failure

I am the bread of life; whoever comes to me shall not hunger, and whoever believes in me shall never thirst.

John 6:35

I am the way and the truth and the life

John 14:6

I can do all things through Christ who strengthens me.

Philippians 4:13

Nothing impossible

The word itself says 'I'm possible

Give thanks always

1 Thessalonians 5:18

"The happiness of your life depends on the quality of your thoughts."

Your word is a lamp for my feet, a light on my path.
Psalms 119:105

You are who you are meant to be...

Live, dance love and dream.

You are the light of the world.

Matthew 5:14

You do not find peace
and happy life

You make them

We love because
he first loved us.

1 John 4:19

Happiness is not something readymade

It comes from your own actions

You shall love your neighbor as yourself.

Mark 12:31

During darkest moments, must focus to see the light.

Let love and faithfulness never leave you.

Proverbs 3:3

Never give up

Great things take time

If you declare
with your mouth,
"Jesus is Lord,"
and believe in your heart
that God raised him
from the dead,
you will be saved.

Just as I have loved you, you also are to love one another.

John 13:34

Don't let other people write your script ♡

For we walk by faith, not by sight.

2 Corinthians 5:7

Everything is possible for one who believes.

Mark 9:23

Our dreams can come true, if we have the courage to pursue them

Made in the USA
Columbia, SC
01 July 2024

37967705R00111